T0051309

A is for Arches

A Utah Alphabet

Written by Becky Hall and Illustrated by Katherine Larson

Sleeping Bear Press™

2395 South Huron Parkway, Suite 200
Ann Arbor, MI 48104
www.sleepingbearpress.com

Printed and bound in the United States.

11 10 9

Library of Congress Cataloging-in-Publication Data

Hall, Rebecca, 1950-
A is for arches : a Utah alphabet book / by Rebecca Hall; illustrated
by Katherine Larson.
p. cm.
Summary: An alphabet book that introduces Utah's history, culture, and
landscape, from Arches National Park to Zion National Park.
ISBN 978-1-58536-096-3
1. Utah—Juvenile literature. 2. English language—Alphabet—Juvenile
literature. [1. Utah. 2. Alphabet.] I. Larson, Katherine, ill. II.
Title.
F826.3 .H27 2003
979.2—dc21   2003010461

For Dave, Sarah, and Brooks

BECKY

❧

Dedicated to the Dudleys—Blair, Di, Ruby, Chase, and Violet—
For bravely lending their images to this book and for their
kindness and friendship through these many years.

KATHERINE

We'll start with Utah's **A**rches,
made from wind, frost, and rain.
Nature's rocky sculptures—
An art that can't remain.

Utah's most famous arches are near Moab at Arches National Park. These are nature's sandstone sculptures, formed by freezing and thawing, by flowing water, and by wind. After many years, arches fall apart because the process that forms them also destroys them. New arches are slowly forming all the time.

The world's longest natural arch is in Utah; it is not clear where, though. The decision depends on the way an arch is measured. Two arches compete for this honor: Landscape Arch (measuring between 291 and 306 feet) in Arches National Park and Kolob Arch (measuring between 292 and 310 feet) in Zion National Park. Some of this measuring was done by hand, and more recently it was done electronically.

The desert ecosystem where these arches are found is unique. The soil can be so fragile that it never recovers from human footsteps. The only poisonous lizard in the United States, the Gila monster, is found here. Other common animals of the area include mule deer, coyote, gray fox, ground squirrels, collared lizards, and rattlesnakes.

a A

The state insect is the honeybee. On the flag, bees buzz around a yellow hive. An early name for the state was "Deseret," which meant honeybee. Utah's nickname is the "Beehive State."

The state motto is "Industry" which means hard work. In 1847 Mormon pioneers settled in Salt Lake City in an attempt to find religious freedom. They had to be resourceful and industrious in order to survive in the harsh desert. They grew their own food, produced as much as they could for themselves, and mined the nearby hills. They tried to be self-sufficient and at one point, they even wanted to be a separate country. Found on the state seal and the flag, it makes sense that "Industry" was chosen in 1959 as Utah's motto.

B b

Busy Bees, that's what we are—
Our symbol is the hive.
From mining to technology,
this helps our state survive.

The rock and mineral of the state,
       Coal and Copper, begin with C.
They're found in mines both north and south.
Come search for them with me.

C
c

The world's first open pit copper mine is near Salt Lake City in Bingham Canyon. Called "The Richest Hole on Earth," it covers more than 1,900 acres and is two and one-half miles wide and three-fourths of a mile deep. Since 1906 over six billion tons of material have been removed, including gold and silver. A mountain once stood where now there is a deep hole.

The state rock is coal, and the mines are located in central and southeastern Utah. Although Brigham Young and his followers started the mines, many of the miners were brought to Utah from Italy, China, Finland, Greece, Japan, and Mexico. That is how such a variety of people from all over the world settled in central Utah.

Utah does have its own Dixie. Before the Civil War began, the state's leader, Brigham Young, wanted Utah to be more independent and produce its own cotton. He did not want to rely on the battling southern states, the original Dixie. In October 1861 he sent settlers to southern Utah to start a new "Dixie" where they could grow cotton. The settlers named their community St. George, after the local leader, George A. Smith. They built a cotton factory that began producing cloth and cotton stuffing by 1867. The factory stayed open until 1910. Today this area is still called Utah's "Dixie."

Did you know there are two Dixies?
Utah has its very own.
Settled in the 1860s,
here cotton once was grown.

E e

Rocky Mountain Elk is **E**.
At Hardware Ranch it's found.
To see this gentle giant beast,
you cannot make a sound.
Sh-h-h!

The state mammal is the Rocky Mountain Elk, which native people called Wapiti. The males or bull elk have antlers that they shed each year. The bulls average six feet in height, nine feet in length, and may weigh as much as 950 pounds. The females are smaller.

The elk live mostly in the mountains, but come into the valleys during the winter, eating grass, leaves, and tender tree branches. At Hardware Ranch in Hyrum the elk are protected. The State Department of Natural Resources feeds as many as 700 elk each winter. This prevents Utah's state mammal from starving and local ranches from losing precious trees and bushes.

Four Corners is the only place in the United States where four states touch. These are Utah, Colorado, New Mexico, and Arizona. They meet on the Navajo Reservation.

F also stands for the Family Research Center in downtown Salt Lake City. It is the number one place in the world for genealogical research. If you want to learn more about your family history, go there or visit their website at www.familysearch.org. They have over two million microfilms of records from more than 97 countries. Many of the records are protected in vaults dug deep into the granite mountainside of Little Cottonwood Canyon outside Salt Lake City.

Ff

F is our Four Corners,
   where four western states all meet.
If you go there any time,
   you'll feel the desert's heat.

G g

The California Gull is **G**,
this gull is Utah's bird.
It saved the settlers' crops—
A tale you may have heard.

In 1848, during the pioneers' first year in the Salt Lake Valley, there was a disastrous June frost. They replanted crops, but crickets swarmed the fields, devouring everything, even nibbling on ladies' cotton skirts. The gulls appeared out of nowhere and ate the bugs, saving the settlers' crops.

Because of this miraculous event, the California gull was proclaimed the Utah state bird in 1955.

Many pioneers pulled or pushed handcarts to Zion, which was an early name for Utah. Ten handcart companies brought 3,000 people from 1856 to 1860. Each cart held 400 to 500 pounds of food, bedding, clothing, and cooking utensils. It took two strong people to pull them. Five people were assigned to each cart. Adults were allowed 17 pounds of personal items and children were allowed 10. A few ox-drawn wagons carried extra baggage, including one public tent for every 20 people.

The pioneers' success proved that using handcarts was an efficient and inexpensive way to move large numbers of people westward.

H is for the Handcarts
the settlers pulled to Zion.
Most folks could not walk that far,
but they just kept on tryin'.

I stands for Irrigation,
it's what the settlers used.
When you live in desert land,
there's not much else to choose.

Irrigation is woven into the history of Utah. When Brigham Young led the first settlers to the Salt Lake Valley, he stressed the importance of water. He encouraged them to grow crops on small parcels of land. Ditches caught the runoff from the mountain snows, and the Water Master, a respected community leader, oversaw the distribution of water. By 1865 the desert bloomed because of the 277 canals that provided water for more than 150,000 acres.

Even today, many towns still have community irrigation. Large water projects have created reservoirs like Flaming Gorge, Glen Canyon, and Lake Powell. These are called "multipurpose river projects" because they are not only used for irrigation of crops but also for recreation, business, flood control, fish, and wildlife.

I i

J j

The Mountain Men, Jim Bridger and Jedediah Smith, were among the first white men to enter Utah. Collecting animal pelts from fall through early summer, in the spring they met other trappers at the Rendezvous, where they sold what they had stored all year. The Rendezvous was a time of celebration. The Mountain Men danced, sang, and competed in foot races and shooting matches. Jim Bridger was famous for telling tall tales around the campfire. Jedediah Smith was known for losing an ear to a bear when it took his head in its mouth.

Even today visitors to Utah can experience the Rendezvous. At Fort Buenaventura people dress in authentic Mountain Men costumes to reenact this spring event.

Jim and Jed, they both are J,
traders and explorers, too.
First white men at Great Salt Lake—
In fall they met at Rendezvous.

In 1982 Dr. Willem Kolff and Dr. Robert Jarvik developed the first human artificial heart. Barney Clark made medical history when he received that heart at the University of Utah. Made of Dacron polyester, plastic, and aluminum, the Jarvik-7 was a system of compressed air hoses that entered the heart through the chest. Barney Clark lived for 16 weeks while a huge machine pumped blood throughout his body. Under Dr. Kolff's direction, the University of Utah has developed one of the world's leading artificial organ research centers.

Kolff and Jarvik designed a heart
which was received by Barney Clark.
For 16 weeks Clark stayed alive.
Now, thanks to them, more folks survive.

ert Jarvik

Dr. Willem Kolff

K k

L is for the Great Salt Lake.
It's saltier than all the rest.
People float like corks in there,
and brine shrimp thrive the best.

The largest salt lake in the western hemisphere, the Great Salt Lake is what remains of Lake Bonneville, an ice age lake that covered much of Utah and parts of Idaho and Nevada. As it evaporated, the salinity or saltiness increased so that today only brine shrimp and bacteria can survive in it. If you have trouble floating, this is the place to go. The lake is four times saltier than the oceans and has enough salt in it to satisfy the world's needs for 1,000 years.

Today visitors drive along the causeway to Antelope Island where they can swim and bob in the water. During the spring and fall, brine shrimp provide food for migrating birds. Depending on the water level, two to five million shorebirds can be seen around the lake during migration. Antelope Island is also an ideal place for wildlife watching. There is a herd of 600 bison. Bighorn sheep, mule deer, pronghorn antelope, and coyotes are also plentiful there.

The Mormon Tabernacle Choir is world famous. Tourists travel to hear the 320 volunteers sing at Temple Square in Salt Lake City. The singers are between the ages of 30 and 60 and are limited to 20 years of service. The choir is known for its weekly radio and television shows, top-selling records (five gold and two platinum albums) and worldwide tours. Begun in 1929, their broadcast is the longest running radio show in history.

The Mormon Tabernacle, the dome-shaped building where the choir has sung for many years, is famous for its excellent acoustics. A pin dropped on the floor can be heard 170 feet away. Since few construction supplies were available in 1863, its builders had to improvise. Instead of nails, they used wooden pegs and rawhide. The pillars appear to be marble. The benches seem to be oak. The organ pipes look like metal, but this is an optical illusion. They were all painted Utah pine.

Mormon Tabernacle Choir—
A group that travels near and far,
    singing songs around the world—
You must learn who they are.

Many tribes in Utah represent Native American Indians. There were prehistoric Fremont and Anasazi, but today Goshute, Navajo, Ute, Paiute, and Shoshone tribal members live in Utah. The state is named after the Ute people. The original name meant "home or location on the mountain top."

Visitors to Utah are delighted by the rock art left behind on canyon walls. The Anasazi's designs and pictures were either chipped into the rock (petroglyphs) or painted on them (pictographs). Their granaries perched high on cliffs, their round ceremonial pits called kivas, and their footprints etched into rock walls are the mysterious remains of a civilization that disappeared from the Four Corners area in Utah almost 800 years ago.

N n

N is for the Native clans,
    ancient and with us today.
Anasazi left behind
    homes and art they made from clay.

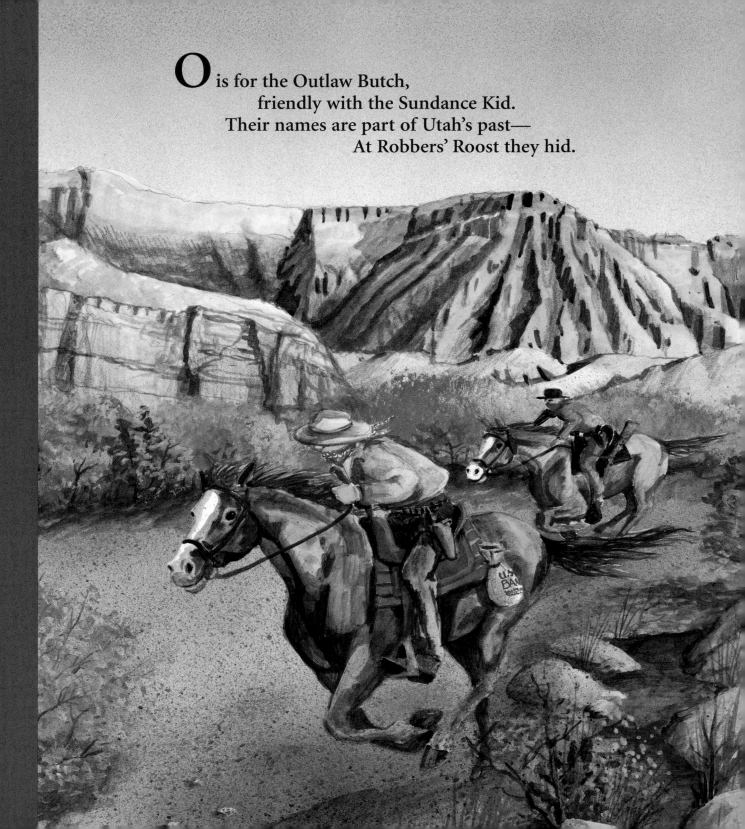

O is for the Outlaw Butch,
      friendly with the Sundance Kid.
Their names are part of Utah's past—
      At Robbers' Roost they hid.

Born in 1866 in Beaver, George Leroy Parker is better known as Butch Cassidy. Like Robin Hood, he supposedly stole from the wealthy and gave to the poor. His hideout, known as Robbers' Roost, was between Hanksville and Moab.

The outlaw trail ran from Mexico to Canada. Because of a distrust of big business and the government, some Utah ranchers were sympathetic toward the outlaws and gave them food and fresh horses.

O is also for Ogden, located north of Salt Lake City. It claims to be the oldest settlement in Utah. Originally known as Fort Buenaventura, it was started as a trading post in 1844-1845 by the mountain man Miles Goodyear.

Pp

The Pony Express began in April 1860 and delivered mail for only 18 months. In that time the riders galloped 650,000 miles on horseback, carried 34,753 pieces of mail, and lost only one mailbag. They traveled from St. Joseph, Missouri, through Utah to Sacramento, California. Every 10 to 15 miles the horses were changed. New riders took over after 75 miles. One time William C. "Buffalo Bill" Cody rode 322 miles in 21 hours and 40 minutes using 21 horses.

In October 1861 the Pony Express ended when the Transcontinental Telegraph was completed and communication improved. Several of the original Pony Express stations can still be seen along the route in the west desert near Callao. At Simpson Springs the station has been reconstructed.

The Pony Express is P.
It started long distance mails.
Riders braved the heat and cold,
and frightening mountain trails.

In 1937 Joe Quinney headed a group of businessmen who formed the Salt Lake City Winter Sports Association. Their plan was to start a ski area for local Utahns. In 1938 Alta's first ski lift was installed. Soon after its opening, a single ride cost 25 cents and a day ticket was $1.50. Some said the area was so expensive that the sport was reserved for the rich. Today Alta is a popular ski resort known for its world-famous powder and fair prices.

In the 1800s Alta was a lively mining town. There were 5,000 residents and 26 saloons! Many other old Utah mining communities like Grafton, Frisco, and Silver Reef are now ghost towns.

Q q

Joe Quinney was a Salt Lake man
who loved the mountain snow.
He helped to start a local spot
where skiers like to go.

R is for the Railroad trains
which met at Promontory.
Connected both the coasts by rail—
Soon people raced to tell the story.

On May 10, 1869, at Promontory Point, the Central Pacific and the Union Pacific Railroads joined after four years of difficult and often dangerous work. Trains then connected the East and West.

In celebration, the governor of California attempted to drive the final spike into the track. After he failed two times, a railroad worker stepped forward and drove the golden spike with one whack. Many photographs recorded the moment, and telegraph messages sent word throughout the country declaring the wonder of the transcontinental railroad.

S is the flower of our state.
It grows where it's not hilly.
The petals are a pearly white—
Its name is Sego lily.

The Sego lily is the Utah state flower. Chosen in 1911 by Utah's schoolchildren, it grows six to eight inches tall on open grasslands. The flower's white petals may have a yellow or pink tinge. The walnut-sized bulbs of the Sego lily were eaten by native populations, and kept many of the pioneers alive in their first years of settlement.

Another **S** is Salt Lake City. Founded by the Mormons in 1847, it is the state's capital. It is the smallest United States city to have a major symphony, three dance companies, and an opera company. It is also home to the professional basketball team, the Utah Jazz.

Our state's gem, topaz is golden or light brown when found in the ground; it becomes colorless in the sunlight. In the United States topaz is commonly found in only three states: New Hampshire, Colorado, and Utah. It is used in jewelry and is almost as hard as a diamond.

Topaz is also the name for the World War II Japanese-American relocation camp. A ghost town today, in 1942 Topaz was "home" to about 9,000 Japanese-American citizens when they were forced to move to this desert location near Delta. Most were American citizens but the United States government feared that they might help Japan during the war. At the end of the war in 1945, all the Japanese prisoners were released, but in the meantime most of them had lost their homes, land, businesses, and possessions.

T is Topaz, Utah's gem.
It sparkles golden brown.
When you place it in the light,
its color can't be found.

Tt

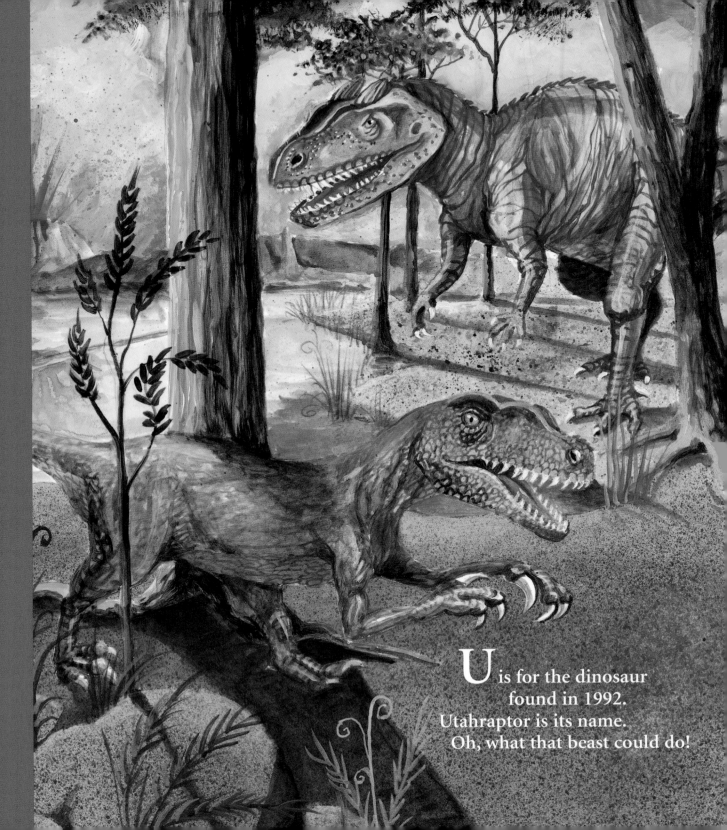

A local rock collector, Robert Gaston, discovered the Utahraptor, which lived 125 million years ago. Described as an "extraordinary killing machine," this carnivorous or meat-eating dinosaur had huge 12-14-inch-long slashing claws and was approximately eight feet tall and twenty feet long. One unusual characteristic of the Utahraptor was that it had four toes, one of which had a long claw that could be retracted when it ran. This way the claw remained sharp for fighting. Scientists think this dinosaur hunted in packs and success-fully attacked larger dinosaurs because of its effective weapons. Found in a remote part of Arches National Park, the Utahraptor's bones are now on display at the College of Eastern Utah in Price.

Our state fossil, Allosaurus, is found more often in Utah than anywhere else in the world. Another carnivorous dinosaur, it roamed here 160 million years ago, and weighed four tons and stood on two legs. It was 17 feet tall, and measured 35 feet long.

U u

U is for the dinosaur
found in 1992.
Utahraptor is its name.
Oh, what that beast could do!

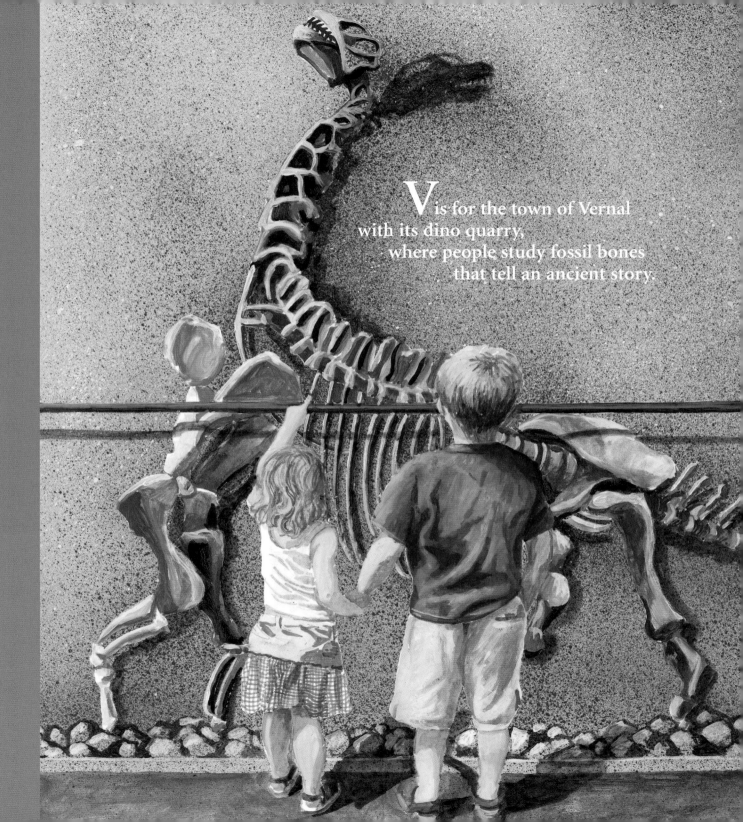

V is for the town of Vernal
with its dino quarry,
where people study fossil bones
that tell an ancient story.

Vernal, near the Colorado border, is where Dinosaur National Monument is located. Scientists uncovered dinosaur bones from the strata or layers at the Dinosaur Quarry. These paleontologists carefully dusted away the dirt to reveal bones from 65 million years ago. Right here the world's most complete dinosaur remains were found.

Long ago this area was an ancient riverbed that probably had quicksand at its bend. Dinosaurs came to drink there and were trapped in the soft sand. Over millions of years their remains that were encased in the sediment became fossils.

From 1909 until 1924, 350 tons of bones and attached rock were removed from the area. This included 23 complete skeletons and parts of hundreds more. The dinosaurs were from six to 84 feet long. After 1924 the bones were no longer removed but simply exposed for visitors to view.

Rising up from the flat desert, the Wasatch Mountains run from the northern boundary to the middle of the state and contain some of the oldest rocks geologists have ever discovered. Some are estimated to be two billion years old. The mountains were formed when the earth's plates moved and cracked (geologic faulting). They also developed from volcanic activity and glaciation. Most of the state's people live along the western edge, called the Wasatch Front. Even today Utahns rely on the mountain snowmelt for their fresh, clear water.

W is also for the Winter Olympic Games held in Utah in February 2002. There were 78 medal events. Salt Lake City is the largest city to ever host the Winter Games.

The Wasatch Mountains loom above,
providing water for the town.
The snow collects all winter long—
In spring it melts and rushes down.

X x

Letter **X** is Xeriscape,
a word that has a funny sound.
Important for the desert folk,
who plant upon the driest ground.

Xeriscape (pronounced zeri-scape) comes from the Greek word "Xeros", which means dry. Xeriscape gardening is conservation of water through creative landscaping. It can mean using plants that are drought tolerant and therefore require little water. This is important in Utah, because the state is the second driest in the country, after Nevada. But Utah does the most watering of all the states, about 250 gallons per person per day. More than 60% of this is for yards.

In a typical yard, 18 gallons of water are used per square foot during the growing season. Drought tolerant plants in the same yard require three gallons of water per square foot.

Now, doesn't xeriscape gardening make sense?

Brigham Young led the Mormon pioneers to Utah after they fled from mobs in Nauvoo, Illinois. He organized and directed the settlement of the Salt Lake Valley. He drew up a plan for a city with irrigation, open spaces, and wide streets. With only two months of real schooling, he was a carpenter, a painter, and a glazier (a person who works with window glass), as well as a smart businessman and a church leader. He enjoyed dancing, theater, and music, and encouraged cultural events. He oversaw the Mormon settlement of many communities in Utah, Nevada, Wyoming, Arizona, and California, making him one of America's most successful colonizers.

Yy

Utah's children know of him,
from Nauvoo he came.
Led the settlers to this place...
And Brigham Young's his name.

Although Zion was an early name for the Mormon settlement, it is also Utah's first National Park, established in 1919. The Virgin River cuts through Zion Canyon which is 2,400 feet deep and one-half mile wide. One famous hike is through the Narrows, where a person can walk upstream and, in places, nearly touch both sides of the canyon with outstretched arms. The ancient Anasazi lived around Zion from 1,500 until 800 years ago. Abandoned cliff houses, rock art, and chipping sites are visible throughout the park. With its variety of landscapes, it is a popular place for visitors from all over the world.

Zion National Park is Z:
Its canyon walls so steep,
pine-filled trails and granite cliffs,
and turquoise skies so deep.

Now your trip 'round Utah's done—
From southern orange desert sand
to northern pine-edged mountain lakes—
Come celebrate this land!

Questions & Answers for Busy Bees!

1. Name the two longest natural arches in the world, which are found in Utah.

2. The only poisonous lizard in the United States can be found in Utah. What is its name?

3. "The Richest Hole on Earth" is found in Bingham Canyon near Salt Lake City. What is it?

4. What is the name of the only place in the United States where four states touch?

5. What is Utah's state mammal?

6. A tale says this state bird saved settlers' crops in 1848. What bird is it?

7. Name the lake that is four times saltier than the world's oceans.

8. This dome-shaped building in Salt Lake City is famous for its world-renowned choir. What is the name of the building?

9. Heart patient Barney Clark made medical history when he received the first human artificial heart at the University of Utah. What was the name of the invention?

10. George Leroy Parker is better known as the outlaw partner of the Sundance Kid. What was his nickname?

11. What is the name of Utah's state flower?

12. Name Utah's state gem, which is golden or light brown when found in the ground and is almost as hard as a diamond.

13. This "killing machine" dinosaur was discovered in 1992 by a Utah rock collector. What is its name?

14. What type of gardening helps conserve water by using plants that need little water? It starts with the letter X.

15. Who was the famous Utah pioneer who organized the first Mormon settlement of the Salt Lake Valley?

Answers

1. Landscape Arch in Arches National Park and Kolob Arch in Zion National Park

2. The Gila monster

3. It is the world's first open pit copper mine and covers more than 1,900 acres and is two and one-half miles wide and three-fourths of a mile deep.

4. Four Corners is where Utah, Colorado, New Mexico, and Arizona meet.

5. The state mammal is the Rocky Mountain Elk.

6. The California Gull is Utah's state bird.

7. The Great Salt Lake

8. The Mormon Tabernacle

9. The Jarvik-7

10. Butch Cassidy

11. Sego lily

12. Topaz is the state gem.

13. The Utahraptor

14. Xeriscape (pronounced zeri-scape)

15. Brigham Young

Becky Hall

Becky Hall is an elementary school teacher and librarian, and lives in Salt Lake City, Utah, with her husband and two children. She is an active member of her local library/media association and the Society of Children's Book Writers & Illustrators. She loves children's bookstores and regularly attends writing workshops. In her free time Becky hikes in the mountains of Utah with her dogs.

Katherine Larson

Katherine Larson sold her first painting at the age of 14. She is currently a classical singer, an illustrator, a muralist, and the owner of Diva Designs in Ann Arbor, Michigan. Her work has taken her across the United States for murals in private homes, institutions, and retail stores. She has done over 350 commissioned paintings for magazines, private owners, businesses, public spaces, and books. *A is for Arches* is Katherine's second book with Sleeping Bear Press. She also illustrated *G is for Grand Canyon: An Arizona Alphabet*.